RAINY DAY

COOKING

DENNY ROBSON
AND
VANESSA BAILEY

FRANKLIN WATTS
LONDON · NEW YORK · TORONTO · SYDNEY

CONTENTS

Salad faces	4
Cinnamon toast	6
Pizza bread	8
Pizza faces	10
Toadstools in grass	13
Pancakes	15
Ginger biscuits	16
Icing biscuits	18
Raspberry ice cream	20
Pastry making	22
Pastry fillings	24
Fairy cakes	26
Icing cakes	28
Peppermint creams	30
Marzipan treats	31
Cook's code and Index	32

Design: David West Children's Book Design
Photography: Roger Vlitos

© Aladdin Books Ltd 1991

Created and designed by
N.W. Books Ltd
28 Percy Street
London W1P 9FF

First published in Great Britain in 1991 by
Franklin Watts Ltd
96 Leonard Street
London EC2A 4RH

ISBN 0-7496-0518-9

A CIP catalogue record for this book is available from the British Library

All rights reserved

Printed in Belgium

Introduction

Cooking your own food and preparing good things to eat can be great fun. In this book you will find lots of ideas for all kinds of food, from funny-faced salads for supper, to delicious tea-time snacks, to mouth-watering sweets to make as presents.

Cooking isn't difficult and it gets easier with practice, but there are some rules you have to learn to be a good cook. The most important is that a good cook is a safe cook, so before you start, read the cook's code on page 31. Remember, safety in the kitchen is a matter of common sense.

Some of the recipes in this book use the oven, others the grill, others need boiling water or sharp knives. **Always check with an adult to see what supervision and help you will need for each recipe before you start.** Once you have learned some of the basic skills, you can start adding your own ideas of what you think will look and taste good to make up your own recipes. Happy cooking!

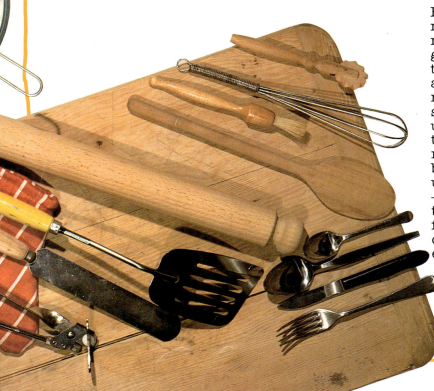

Before you start, read the recipe right through and get together all the ingredients and utensils you need. Here are some of the utensils we used to make the recipes in this book. Try to wash up as you go along — it's much better than having to face a huge pile of dirty dishes at the end!

Salad faces

Salads make perfect lunches in summer when no one wants to eat a hot meal, but prepare them with a bit of imagination and they can look tempting at any time of year. Vary the ingredients each time you make them. Celery, apple, raisins and white cabbage make a change from lettuce and tomato. Look around the supermarkets for unusual fruits and mix different flavours together. Experiment with dips to go with the salads — use yoghurt or mayonnaise mixed with other ingredients.

WHAT YOU NEED
Really fresh vegetables and fruits, such as plums, apples, oranges or bananas (try also mango, kiwi and star fruit), lettuce (there are lots of different kinds to choose from), tomatoes, peppers or spring onions, chopping board
sharp knife
two plates

1 Wash and dry the fruits and vegetables. To wash lettuce, first discard the coarse outer leaves, separate the others, wash in cold water and shake dry in a tea towel.

2 Cut up fruit to make the fruity face. Put a damp tea towel under the chopping board to make sure it doesn't slip and use a small sharp knife.

3 We have used cheese and a radish for the green man's nose, slices of hard-boiled egg and olives for his eyes, and cheese for hair. You could also roll up ham 'curls' for hair.

FRUITY FACE

GREEN MAN

Cinnamon toast

Hot buttered toast makes a satisfying snack to keep you going after school, but you can turn it into a real treat if you add something special to it. Spread toast with mashed banana sprinkled thickly with brown sugar and then put it back under the grill until the sugar starts to melt. Or try toast with a slice of cheese melting over ham or a pineapple ring. Here we show you how to make cinnamon toast. Cinnamon shapes taste delicious and look good enough to be served up as party food.

WHAT YOU NEED
slices of bread
butter
brown sugar
ground cinnamon
saucepan
spoon
shape cutters
bowl

1 Mix 1 tablespoonful of cinnamon with 3 tablespoonfuls of sugar and 50 gr (2 oz) of butter in a bowl. Place the bowl in a saucepan of water. Stir over a low heat until you have a paste. Taste and add more sugar if desired.

2 Toast the bread on one side only. Spread the cinnamon paste generously on the untoasted side and then pop it back under the grill until it is hot.

3 When the toast is cool enough to handle, cut out shapes with cutters if you have them, or use a sharp knife if you don't.

4 Eat the shapes while they are still warm and don't forget you can eat the leftovers too!

1 Put the sugar and yeast in a bowl, add the warm water and stir well to blend. Put in a warm place for 10-15 minutes.

2 Sift the flour into a bowl, add the salt and rub in the fat with your fingertips. (See page 22 for how to do this.)

3 Add the dissolved yeast liquid to the flour and stir with a wooden spoon until it makes a dough. Knead it in the bowl for a couple of minutes.

WHAT YOU NEED
To make 6 pizzas:
300 gr (12 oz) wholewheat or strong white flour
25 gr (1 oz) butter or lard
1 tbsp dried yeast
200 ml (7 fl oz) warm water
1 tsp salt
1 tsp sugar
mixing bowl
measuring jug
scales
chopping board
rolling pin
wooden spoon
baking tray

Pizza bread

A pizza is an Italian dish consisting of a round bread base covered with tomato, cheese and other savoury items. Pizzas make excellent lunch or tea-time dishes served with salad and because they can have a whole variety of toppings, they are usually everyone's favourite. Here we show you how to make real pizza bread, but you could make quick pizzas by using toasted bread bun halves, french bread, pitta bread or crumpets for the base. You can also use the recipe below to make bread rolls or loaves.

Kneading
You knead bread dough to improve the texture of the dough and also to strengthen it before baking. Put the dough on to a floured surface and shape it into a ball. Fold the dough towards you, push down with the heel of your hand and away with your palm. Give the dough a quarter turn, fold the dough towards you and repeat.

4

4 Put the dough on to a lightly floured chopping board and knead it well until it is smooth and elastic. This will take about ten minutes. Cover it with a tea towel and then leave it in a warm place for about an hour until it has risen.

5 Knead the dough again for a few minutes on a lightly floured surface. Divide the dough into 6 pieces and roll each out to make a circle about 1 cm thick.

6 You can use a plate to help you make the shape. Make a small rim on each pizza base.

5

6

7 Oil a baking tray for the pizza bases. They are now ready for the toppings.

7

Pizza faces

WHAT YOU NEED
tomato puree
cheese (mozzarella is best)
tomatoes
herbs
olives
other ingredients as desired, such as:
ham
slices of salami
peppers
anchovies

There are lots of things you can put on your pizzas and, as you can see from our photographs, there are lots of ways in which you can decorate them. Make funny pizza faces — olives become eyes, a cherry tomato can be a nose and a slice of pepper gives your pizza a smile. When you have added the toppings, bake the pizzas in a pre-heated hot oven (220°C/425°F, Gas Mark 7) for about 20 minutes or until the pizza base is golden and the cheese has melted.

Spread a layer of tomato puree over the dough. Add grated cheese or slices of mozzarella and finish with the toppings of your choice.

PIZZA CAT
This delicious looking cat is ready to go into the oven. It has herby hair, olive eyes and spring onions for whiskers.

FUNNY FRED
This strange looking character has tomato puree hair and spectacles, olive eyes, green pepper lips and a large tomato nose!

1 Melt 50 gr (2 oz) chocolate by breaking it up and placing it in a bowl over a pan of hot water. Pour it into your serving dish.

2 Cut the banana 'stalks' and brush them with lemon to stop them from going brown.

3 Stand the bananas in the melted chocolate. If they won't stand upright, you could tape them as shown below.

4 Make up the jelly according to the instructions on the packet.

5 When it has cooled a little, carefully pour the liquid jelly around the banana stalks.

6 Paint the meringues with red food colouring to make the toadstool tops.

7 Spread a little golden syrup or honey on the top of each banana 'stalk' and stick a meringue top on each.

Toadstools in grass

WHAT YOU NEED
green jelly
meringues
chocolate
bananas
honey or golden syrup
a lemon
red food colouring
saucepan
glass bowl
measuring jug
serving dish
wooden spoon
paint brush

Colourful desserts made with jellies are always popular. Make up a jelly with half water and half fruit-flavoured yoghurt and you have a delicious creamy jelly. Use two different coloured jellies, chop them up when set, layer them in tall glasses with fruit, top with ice cream and you have a mouth-watering stripey sundae. Here we show you a rather exotic jelly dessert which is great fun to make.

Quick setting jelly
The quickest way to make a jelly is to first dissolve the cubes in a measuring jug with 150 ml (5 fl oz) of boiling water. When the jelly has dissolved, make it up to 570 ml (20 fl oz) with ice cubes and cold water. This brings the temperature down quickly and so speeds up the setting time.

1 Sift the flour into a bowl, add the salt, make a deep well in the centre and drop in the egg.

2 Gradually stir the flour into the egg.

3 Add a little milk to keep the mixture smooth. Pour in the rest of the milk and beat the mixture well.

4 Stir in one tablespoonful of vegetable oil. Leave to stand for an hour before using.

5 Add a little oil to the frying pan and heat until it is hot. Add enough batter to coat the pan when you tilt it.

Cook until the underside is golden brown and then, using a palette knife, turn it over and cook for another minute.

Pancakes

Pancakes are made from a batter, which is a mixture of flour, milk and eggs that has been beaten to take in lots of air. Pancakes taste equally good with sweet or savoury toppings. Serve them simply sprinkled with lemon and sugar, or cover them with chocolate sauce and whipped cream. They are also delicious rolled and filled with savoury ingredients, like cheese and ham, or a herby onion and tomato mixture.

WHAT YOU NEED
100 gr (4 oz) plain flour
1 egg
250 ml (9 fl oz) milk
vegetable oil
pinch of salt
toppings of your choice
mixing bowl
wooden spoon
small frying pan
palette knife

7 Fold the pancake, sprinkle it with sugar if desired and eat it while it's warm.

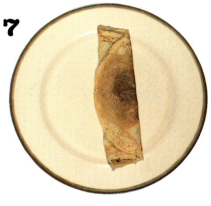

7

6 Carefully remove the pancake from the pan and cover with the topping of your choice.

6

WAFFLES
Waffles are also made with a simple batter mixture, but you make them in a special waffle iron. Eat them with butter, jam, honey, whipped cream, maple syrup or simply dusted with icing sugar.

WHAT YOU NEED
To make a simple batter for 6 waffles:
225 gr (8 oz) plain flour
1 egg
225 ml (8 fl oz) milk
a pinch of salt

1 Sift the flour into a mixing bowl. Add the baking powder, ground ginger and bicarbonate of soda.

2 Melt the butter, sugar and golden syrup in a saucepan over a low heat and pour into the flour mixture.

WHAT YOU NEED
225 gr (8 oz) plain flour
1 tsp baking powder
2 tsp ground ginger
½ tsp bicarbonate of soda
75 g (3 oz) butter
75 g (3 oz) brown sugar
2 tbsp golden syrup
mixing bowl
saucepan
wooden spoon
rolling pin
cutters or sharp knife
palette knife
baking tray

Ginger biscuits

Gingerbread men have been popular biscuits for hundreds of years. Stories have even been written about them. You may know the old tale in which the gingerbread man escapes from the oven, shouting:

Run, run as fast as you can,
You can't catch me I'm the gingerbread man!
This recipe shows you how to make about 20 gingerbread characters.

3 Mix the ingredients in the bowl with a wooden spoon to form a dough. Put the dough on a lightly floured board and knead it lightly. Roll it out to ½ cm thickness.

4 Cut out gingerbread men and any other shapes. Put them on a greased baking tray and bake in the centre of a pre-heated oven (200°C/400°F, Gas Mark 6) for 10-15 minutes.

Icing biscuits

Traditional gingerbread men have currant eyes and buttons which you add before baking, but it can be fun to decorate your gingerbread shapes with icing. After baking, wait until the biscuits are cool and firm and then transfer to a cooling tray where they can become cold and crisp. They are now ready for decorating.

WHAT YOU NEED
icing sugar
hot water
food colouring
decorations such as:
glacé cherries, hundreds and thousands, chocolate strands or angelica
a sieve
mixing bowl
spoon and knife

MAKING GLACÉ ICING

1 For each colour of icing, sift 50gr (2 oz) of icing sugar into a bowl and add 2 teaspoons of water (or fruit juice). Mix well and add more liquid or icing sugar, depending on the consistency you want.

2 Add one or two drops of food colouring and mix in well. Use a knife to decorate your shapes. (Keep dipping it in a glass of hot water to make the icing spread smoothly.) Add the other decorations while the icing is still wet so that they stick.

Raspberry ice cream

WHAT YOU NEED
One 400gr (14 oz) can of evaporated milk
100 gr (4 oz) icing sugar
450 gr (1 lb) fresh or frozen raspberries
mixing bowl
whisk
freezer container

Everyone loves ice cream. Here we show you a simple recipe that is very easy to make. What's more, you can vary the recipe to suit your taste. Make it with strawberries or other soft summer fruits, or stir in candied fruit peel to make Tutti Frutti. It's also delicious combined with other things. Serve it surrounded by sliced bananas and covered with melted chocolate for a banana-raspberry-chocolate split.

Pureeing ingredients
When you make a puree of an ingredient you turn it into a smooth mixture. You can do this by either beating, blending with an electric blender or by rubbing the ingredients through a sieve.

1 Chill the can of milk overnight and then beat it until it is thick and frothy. Beat the icing sugar into the evaporated milk.

2 Make a puree out of the raspberries, either by liquidising them in a blender or by rubbing them through a sieve.

3 Stir the raspberry puree into the milk and icing sugar mixture.

4 Pour it into a freezer container and put it in a freezer or the ice making compartment of a refrigerator.

5 Stir the mixture from time to time while it is freezing. Cover it and it should keep in the freezer for several weeks.

1 Sieve the flour into a mixing bowl and add the salt. Cut the margarine and lard into pieces and add to the flour.

2 With the tips of your fingers, rub the fats into the flour until the mixture resembles fine breadcrumbs.

3 Stir the water into the mixture and bind it together.

Pastry making

Like bread making, lots of people find making pastry a very satisfying part of cooking because you use your hands in its preparation. Pastry can be used in many different dishes, from jam tarts to savoury pies, so it's worth practising until you can make a good light pastry.

Rubbing in
Rubbing in is a technique you use with pastry (and some cake and bread mixtures) where the fat has to be blended evenly with the flour. This has to be done lightly and so you use the tips of your fingers and not your palms. Lift the mixture high and rub with your fingertips to blend. Let the mixture fall back to the bowl and repeat until the fat and flour are blended together and the mixture looks like fine breadcrumbs.

WHAT YOU NEED
225 gr (8 oz) plain flour
50 gr (2 oz) lard
50 gr (2 oz) margarine
pinch of salt
2 – 3 tbsp very cold water
mixing bowl
rolling pin
floured board
baking tray or pastry tins
pastry cutter

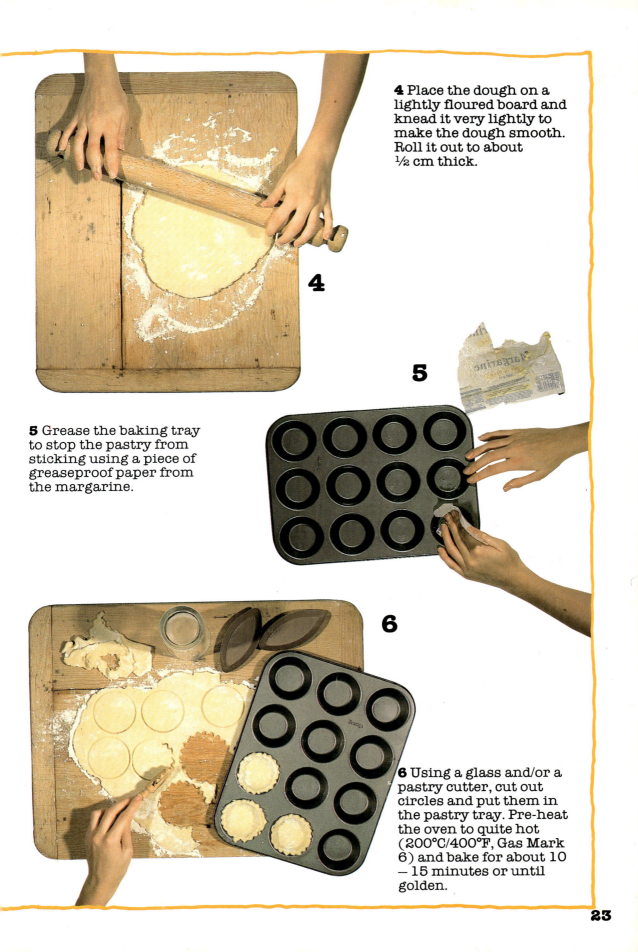

4 Place the dough on a lightly floured board and knead it very lightly to make the dough smooth. Roll it out to about ½ cm thick.

5 Grease the baking tray to stop the pastry from sticking using a piece of greaseproof paper from the margarine.

6 Using a glass and/or a pastry cutter, cut out circles and put them in the pastry tray. Pre-heat the oven to quite hot (200°C/400°F, Gas Mark 6) and bake for about 10 – 15 minutes or until golden.

Pastry fillings

You could fill your pastry cases quite simply by adding a spoonful of your favourite jam, or you could turn them into desserts by filling them with whipped cream and fruit. Savoury tarts are also delicious. Experiment with different fillings, like tuna mixed with peppers and tomato, or egg mixed with creamy mayonnaise.

Whipping cream
Whipped cream always makes a dessert special. Cream is whipped to thicken it and to increase its volume. You can use a simple hand whisk, although this takes quite a bit of effort, a rotary hand whisk or an electric one.

When the pastry cases are cooked, let them cool a little and then turn them out on to a wire cooling tray until completely cold. They are now ready for filling.

We turned our round pastry cases into jam tarts by filling them with apricot, raspberry and strawberry jams.

The oval pastry cases are now mouth-watering dessert boats, filled with tinned fruit cocktail and whipped cream.

Fairy cakes

WHAT YOU NEED
100 gr (4 oz) margarine
100 gr (4 oz) caster sugar
2 eggs, beaten
100 gr (4 oz) self-raising flour
small cake cases
mixing bowl
sieve
wooden spoon
baking tray

You can use this basic cake recipe to make a whole range of different cakes. Substitute a quarter of the flour for cocoa powder and you can make a chocolate cake. Divide the mixture between two cake tins, bake, fill with cream and jam and this is a Victoria Sandwich cake. But perhaps nicest of all are fairy cakes because you can have fun icing them in lots of different ways.

Creaming ingredients

Creaming is a technique mainly used in cake making and it means to blend ingredients together until they are soft and light and fluffy. This is always best done with a wooden spoon.

1 Put the sugar into a basin and add the margarine. Break the margarine up into pieces and then cream the two together, beating with a wooden spoon until the mixture is light and fluffy.

2 Start adding some of the beaten eggs, along with a little of the flour to prevent the mixture curdling.

3 Continue adding the eggs and the sifted flour, a little of each at a time, blending them together with a wooden spoon.

4 Beat well for a minute until the mixture is smooth and creamy.

5 Place the cake cases well apart on a baking tray. Spoon a small amount of mixture into each. Bake in a moderate oven (180°C/350°F, Gas Mark 4) until the cakes are risen and golden brown.

Icing cakes

No party tea is complete without a plateful of colourful iced fairy cakes. Decorate them with glacé icing (see page 18) or use creamy butter icing. To make this, cream 50 gr (2 oz) butter in a basin until soft, beat in 75 gr (3 oz) sifted icing sugar, a little at a time, until the mixture is smooth. Divide it up and add food colourings.

Cool the cakes on a wire rack before decorating. To turn them into butterfly cakes, slice off the tops, cut them in two and replace in icing.

WHAT YOU NEED
- butter
  icing sugar
  food colourings
  decorations such as:
  Smarties, glacé cherries,
  hundreds and thousands,
  angelica, chocolate
  strands

1 Pour the milk into a basin. Carefully add just a few drops of peppermint essence and green food colouring.
2 Sift the icing sugar into the basin and stir until the mixture is quite stiff.
3 Sprinkle some cornflour on to a board. This will stop the mixture sticking. Put the mixture on the board and knead it until it is smooth.
4 Roll out the mixture to ½ cm thick sheet.
5 Cut out rounds that are about 2 cm across.
6 Dip them in melted chocolate, (see page 12), and when the sweets are dry, wrap them in silver foil.

PEPPERMINT CREAMS
50 ml (2 fl oz) sweetened condensed milk
peppermint essence
green food colouring
200 gr (7 oz) icing sugar
cornflour

Peppermint creams

Making sweets is one of the nicest aspects of cooking. It's fun, easy and the results are usually delicious. Sweets also make perfect presents to give at Christmas-time or for birthdays. If you want to give them as gifts, decorate a suitable box, line it with doilies and place greaseproof paper between the layers of sweets. This recipe is for peppermint creams, but you could also use it to make lemon creams by substituting lemon flavouring and colouring.

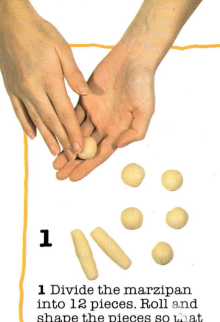
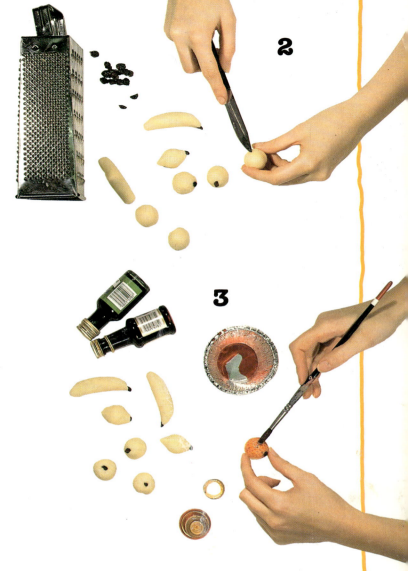

1 Divide the marzipan into 12 pieces. Roll and shape the pieces so that they look like miniature oranges, apples, lemons (pinch the ends to make the lemon shape), pears and bananas.
2 Gently rub the 'oranges' and 'lemons' on the side of a fine grater to give the markings of lemon and orange peel. Make a dent and put a raisin or clove on each fruit to look like a stalk.
3 Use food dyes to colour the fruits.

MARZIPAN FRUITS
50 gr (2 oz) marzipan
food colourings
raisins or cloves

Marzipan treats

Here we show you how to make marzipan fruits. You could also try marzipan whirls. First divide the marzipan into three. Work different food colourings into two of the parts, a drop at a time. Roll each piece out flat and then sandwich the three parts together. Roll up the 'sandwich' into a sausage shape and cut off slices to make the individual sweets.

Cook's code

Before you make anything, check first with an adult to see what help and supervision you may need. Never do any cooking when you are alone in the house.

Always wash your hands before you make anything and wear an apron.

Read the recipe right through before you start, to make sure you have everything you need. Also check the recipe and set the oven at the appropriate temperature.

Measure your ingredients carefully — your recipes can't work if they contain the wrong amounts of ingredients. Measure liquid ingredients in a measuring jug and dry ingredients on kitchen scales.

Use dry oven gloves every time you handle hot saucepan handles or anything from the oven or grill — wet oven gloves let the heat through.

Make sure pan handles are turned towards the back of the cooker away from you so that they don't get knocked accidentally. Make sure no handle is above the heat of another ring.

Always use a chopping board when cutting, preferably on a wet tea towel to stop it slipping. **Watch your fingers.** A small knife is easier to handle than a large one.

Concentrate on what you are doing and don't play around — accidents can happen quite easily.

Wipe up any spills as they happen and clean up the dishes as you go along.

Index

bread 8, 9
bread dough 8, 9

cakes 26, 27, 29
cinnamon toast 6
cook's code 3, 32
creaming 26, 27

desserts 13
dips 4
dough 8, 9, 22-25

fairy cakes 26-29
Fruity Face 5

ginger biscuits 16-19
Green Man 5

ice cream 20, 21
icing 28, 29
icing biscuits 18, 19

jellies 13

kneading 8

marzipan fruits 31
marzipan whirls 31

pancakes 14, 15
pastry 22-25
peppermint creams 30
pizza faces 10, 11

raspberry ice cream 20, 21
rubbing in 22, 23

safety 3, 32
salad faces 4, 5
sweets 30, 31

toadstools in grass 12, 13

waffles 15
whipping cream 24, 25